Big Joe vs. Scratch

Big Joe vs. Scratch

Based on a True Story

By

Philander Whittlesee

The names and details of persons and places in this book have been changed.

ISBN: 979-86-93848-04-7 (print)
ASIN: B08KTWDS9Z (print)
ASIN: B08KZ4F8S5 (ebook)

Edited by Jagi Wright

Cover art by Philander Whittlesee

For Abigail,

Sebastian,

Catherine,

Olivia,

Augustine,

and Daniel

Big Joe

GRAB A SEAT, PARDNER, and take a load off, while I tell you about the time Big Joe met Scratch himself. I'm sure you've heard lots of tales about the devil before, about contracts, and fiddles, and all kinds of things. This story, however, is different from most of them. That's because this story is true. One hundred percent absolutely true.

Now Big Joe was a mountain of a man. He was tall, barrel-chested, and he was loved by all in his community. His parents were teachers and long-time, staunch Democrats, as was he. He was a beacon, a tower, in the small Texas town where he taught Math and History at the local high school, as well as coaching the football and basketball teams. Joe was a minor celebrity in the small community. Everyone knew him; the students and players looked up to him; he was the life of any party, and more than anything else he considered himself a fun guy.

One day just a couple of years ago, with just two days remaining in the school year, Joe was heading home after school. He tossed his gear into the back of his Toyota Camry the same way he always did, but this time he felt something pop in his back. It was just a small thing, a twinge, a click, and nothing that he wasn't familiar with. He was used to little aches and pains. He was a big man; he was active, and as a coach he was familiar with dings and nicks. He would get back pains from time to time, and he knew he would probably be sore for a few days.

By the time Joe got home, his back was hurting him pretty good. He had just two days of classes left to get through. He had been chosen by the senior class to be an honor guard for graduation (his tenth year running), and then he could relax. He just needed to get through these few remaining days. Big Joe was a big, tough guy. He could handle a little back pain.

Now Joe had a peculiar way to diagnose any ache or pain to determine if it might be serious or not. It had never failed him before, and he decided to put it into action once more. Joe's plan was simple. Get rip-roaring drunk. If the pain went away, then it wasn't a problem. If the pain persisted, then it may be a big deal; and he might need to see a doctor.

As fortune would have it, Joe had a case of wine he had ordered waiting for him at the Walgreens drop-off location for UPS. So Joe headed over to Walgreens and picked it up just as he always had. He could have grabbed a cart for the box, but he was a big man who wasn't going to wimp out on an everyday activity like this. Joe had his image to live up to, and his pride, so he hefted the box and held it in front of him.

Picking up the box nearly did Joe in. His back screamed at him. He felt like he had been stabbed. His usual brisk stride was not possible, but Joe wasn't going to be humbled by anything so trivial as mere human frailty; so he gritted his teeth and grunted it out. He started out OK, putting one foot in front of the other, but he wasn't able to move very quickly. By the time he reached the front door, his gait had devolved to more of an ambitious waddle. Still, he made it to the car, pried the door open in an awkward squat while trying to keep his back straight, and then tried to carefully set the box down on the seat. As he bent over, it felt like he was hit with a cattle-prod from behind. He half-dropped the box onto the seat, grasped the door with one hand and the roof frame with the other, and struggled to hold himself upright as he slowly straightened up.

Joe gritted his teeth and felt his lungs bellow and his diaphragm clench every bit as hard as his hands were gripping the metal of the car as he laboriously pulled himself upright. Getting into the front seat was more of a fall and flop than a cautious sitting, but he managed it; and he was able to drive himself home. Once home, Joe started drinking. After having finished several bottles, the pain still wasn't receding. In fact, it was getting worse.

Pondering his situation in his diminishing sobriety, Joe decided that maybe what he really needed was to take some weight off and get into the pool. Let the water relax him, let his body float, and let the evening rays of the early summer sun soak into him and melt the pain away. He took the wine and corkscrew with him, of course, now drinking straight from the bottle.

Eventually, Joe's roommate Rob came home and saw him in the pool. He saw three bottles of wine near the pool and three more in the house in the kitchen.

"Joe, what the hell are you doing in the pool? And why are you drinking wine out here by the bottle?"

"Rob, it's fine," Joe said. "My back hurts, really bad." Joe explained the situation to his friend, ending with, "I need another bottle of wine."

"No, you don't," Rob said. "You need to take some Advil and stop acting like a drunken barbarian."

Rob managed to coax Joe into the house and into bed, where he took some ibuprofen. Laying down, though, hurt Joe badly. Each breath brought a sharp pain, and he felt like his back was trying to murder him. But even with the pain, he passed out.

When he awoke the next morning, things had gotten worse. Joe was in agony. He couldn't move. He hurt so bad he couldn't think. He was desperate and started taking ibuprofen. It didn't help, so he took some more. It still didn't make a difference, so he took more still. Joe took twenty-seven pills of ibuprofen that day, a total of 5400 milligrams, trying to function. He was able to fight through that day and the next, the last day of school, eating ibuprofen like candy. His fellow teachers saw how much pain he was in; and they suggested he see a doctor, but Joe declined.

At home, his roommate saw the condition he was in. He suggested he go to the hospital. Joe didn't want to. Later, when his girlfriend saw him, she wanted to call 911 and get him an ambulance, but again, Joe didn't want to go.

"I'm fine," he said. "It's just tweaked. It'll get better with a few days of rest."

But Joe was scared. He didn't want to go to see any doctor. He feared what they might find with his back, and he was scared about any number of other issues they may discover with his health due to his weight. He was scared about a lot of things, and he knew he wasn't healthy mentally or physically. But it was time to fix that. He was going to tough it out.

The following day, he was even worse. Joe could barely move about the house. Graduation was out. He called his principal and let him know he wouldn't be able to make the practice walkthrough and couldn't make graduation either. He told him he couldn't walk, couldn't stand, and couldn't sit. Joe wanted to feel guilty about it, but he couldn't. He hurt too much to feel guilty.

Over the next several days, Joe deteriorated. He couldn't eat. He could barely drink. The ibuprofen stopped working, so he stopped taking it. His roommate became more and more concerned, along with his girlfriend, and they convinced him to let them call 911 and get him an ambulance.

When the paramedics arrived, they gave him a quick, yet thorough, examination. His vitals were fine. His blood pressure was a little high, but everything else was fine; and as they went over his symptoms and medical history, they said it sounded like he had a pinched nerve. They wanted him to see a doctor, and as much pain as he was in, they wanted it to happen sooner rather than later. But now that Joe understood he wasn't in any danger of immediate death or harm, he no longer felt any urgency to go. Joe declined transport to the hospital.

Joe's girlfriend, Anita, was pretty upset by this decision, but, ultimately, she decided that she didn't live there, wouldn't hear him groaning in pain, and that he was a big boy and could take care of himself. So she left him to his choice. She said she would return in the morning, and then she left the house.

The next two days, Saturday and Sunday, were a blur. Anita tried to help take care of Joe, but he was not a good patient. He wouldn't eat; he couldn't sleep; he could barely take care of himself in the bathroom. But his girlfriend insisted that he eat something and even made him scrambled eggs with toast. Joe gave in and ate the scrambled eggs because she was so insistent and because they reminded him of his childhood, but he refused to eat anything else.

After "Agony Saturday" turned into "Agony

Sunday," Joe knew he had to do something. He would have done anything to ease his pain, or almost anything. Monday, however, was Memorial Day, and everything was closed. Again, Joe tried to tough it out at home.

On Tuesday, Joe called a friend at a local chiropractor. They knew him well and often worked with other individuals from the school athletic program. Joe spoke with the wife of the husband-and-wife chiropractic team, and they were glad to hear from him. However, they were booked solid and only saw new patients on Thursdays. So, Joe scheduled an appointment. After hanging up with them, he continued to dwell in his own personal, private hell for another two days.

When Thursday finally did arrive, it took everything Joe had to make it to the appointment. He had never been to a chiropractor before, and it seemed they made good progress. There was lots of popping and cracking occurring in his neck and spine. The practitioner asked him where it was hurting the worst, and it didn't take too long to find the area and make adjustments. At first, the agony ramped up beyond what Joe could have even believed was possible, even after living through the worst, most pain-filled week of his entire life. He gasped and wanted to scream, but he had no air with which to do so. Instead, laying there, he felt the pain begin to subside. As the relief started to take hold, Joe started to relax. He started to feel good.

The chiropractor told him that with pinched nerves, the pain was likely to come back, and he would probably need several sessions to provide some long-term, positive improvement. Joe understood, and they scheduled an appointment for the following day.

Within about thirty-five minutes, Joe felt the pain come rushing back. It hit him hard and fast, and it came back stronger than before. But Joe expected this. He was hurting and hurting badly, but he knew this was part of the plan. This was expected. He struggled to deal with the pain back home, alone, but he knew everything was going to be OK. He was going to get better.

The following day he returned, as scheduled, for his second adjustment. Again, he was provided relief by the practitioner, but the relief was much shorter-lived than last time. Within fifteen minutes he was in excruciating agony. But again, this was acknowledged as normal, and part of the plan. As it was Friday, they booked another appointment for Monday, and Joe struggled, painfully and slowly, back home.

Time seemed to stretch on interminably. The hours passed. Some passed quickly, some passed so slowly that one could live an entire life in one, and all of this happened seemingly haphazardly, randomly. But Joe knew it was all going to be alright. He was getting better. He was receiving treatment.

The Monday appointment with the chiropractor came and went, and this time the pain was relieved for only five minutes. Each time the pain came back, it was worse than it had been before. The chiropractor was starting to become concerned.

"You should be feeling better by now. Why don't you come back tomorrow for one more session, and we'll see if there is any improvement, or if we have to look at a different option?"

Joe agreed and came back for his fourth appointment on Tuesday. The adjustment did not make a difference. If anything, it made the pain worse. The chiropractor looked at Joe with concern.

"Joe, I would not be doing my job if I didn't tell you that you need to seek other medical attention," he said. "This is not helping."

Joe knew he needed to follow up with his primary care doctor. But Joe hadn't seen his doc in several years. He didn't want to hear again how he needed to lose weight. He didn't want to face the look, the disapproval when he got off the scale. He didn't want to hear again how his weight was putting his health in jeopardy. Joe didn't need any of that right now. He didn't want to sit through a lecture. He feared what they might say.

Instead, Joe went to the local urgent care. They gave him a workup and saw that his vitals weren't bad. They heard his story about how much it hurt and how he had seen the chiropractor and it hadn't fixed anything. They saw how desperate he was. They treated him like they do so many others who come in off the street in pain, desperately looking for relief. They didn't believe him.

Instead, they diagnosed him with anxiety. They thought the pain may be in his head, and they wrote him a script for an anti-anxiety med. Joe was so desperate for any kind of relief from the pain, he didn't argue. He didn't say they were wrong. And who knows? He did have anxiety about seeing his doctor. So, he took the prescription, had it filled, and immediately went home to try it.

Of course, the first pill didn't make a difference at all. Joe didn't let that give him any pause. Three more chased the first one in rapid succession.

In his youth, Joe had done his fair amount of experimentation with narcotics. He knew what it was to be high. Joe got high. He got as high as he had ever been in his life. He got higher. And finally, finally, Joe got the relief he had been seeking. In his mind-altered state, the pain finally disappeared.

Joe had camped out on the couch in his house with his roommate and his girlfriend. He laughed. He giggled. He cried. He guffawed.

"I'm fine! I'm great! The pain is gone!"

But his roommate and his girlfriend knew he couldn't live like this for long. The meds weren't going to last, and he couldn't just stay high for the rest of his life.

Eventually the meds wore off, and in the crash, the pain came back worse than ever. But Joe wasn't fazed. He simply took some more pills. But the pills couldn't keep the pain away this time. It was still there. They pushed it back some but couldn't banish it entirely. No matter how many pills Joe took, the pain remained, and indeed, the pain was again slowly increasing. In just a couple of days, Joe was again unable to ease the pain at all with the anti-anxiety drugs, so he stopped taking them.

Joe didn't move from the couch anymore. He had more-or-less permanently taken over one corner of it. He just tried to survive the new hell he was in. The TV was on, and he would flip through the channels, but he couldn't focus on the TV. It was just noise and lights to help the time flow by. His favorite movie couldn't hold his interest. There was nothing funny about any of the comedies. There was no entertainment and no diversion to be found in the glowing pixels on the screen.

The evening wore on. Joe still couldn't sleep. It just hurt too much. He was suddenly aware there was a Christian preacher on the tube, and he was in the middle of a pretty good spiel.

"Why the hell do I have a televangelist on my TV?" Joe thought to himself. "My God," he continued in disgust.

He was familiar with Christianity. He had been raised in a nominally Christian household and was baptized at a young age. His parents were Christian, and he remembered vividly, and hated, the three-hour Sunday School sessions he had endured as a kid, followed by an hour or two of sermons.

His girlfriend, Anita, was Catholic. Early on in their relationship, she had informed him that if this was ever going to work long-term, he was going to need to attend Mass with her every Sunday, or at least every Sunday that he didn't have a good reason to get out of. During coaching season, it was easier to find obstacles to keep him away.

So, Joe had attended Mass with Anita on most Sundays. It made it easier to deal with that Mass was always only an hour long each weekend, regardless of the occasion. It was a long hour, but he endured it every week. He didn't want to be there; but he went because his girlfriend required it of him, and it earned him brownie points with her. He enjoyed the Easter and Christmas services with the decorations and music, but he never participated. He would sit there in the pew. He never felt worthy of more. He never really believed it to be true.

Joe's pain reared its ugly head again at that moment, and all thought of the preacher departed his head. He glanced at his watch. It was only 3:00 AM. This night was never going to end. But Joe wasn't feeling well. He was in a lot of pain, too, but he was starting to feel downright terrible. It was a struggle to keep conscious. He wondered why he was trying to keep conscious instead of falling asleep, and in a moment of clarity, he knew.

"I'm going to die," he thought.

He knew it to be absolutely and completely true. Deep in his bones and in his heart, he grasped the fundamental, trustworthy nature of that thought.

"I'm going to die, right now."

Joe struggled to desperately cling to consciousness. He knew with absolute, unerring certainty that if he fell asleep now, if he lost consciousness in any way, he would never regain it.

The pain, oh the pain, and the exhaustion... it was too much to bear. But the fear... the fear was real too. Suddenly Joe felt very, very certain that he should not die right now. It was imperative that he not give in. He must cling to life.

Now time started to move, once again flowing rapidly, or at least seemingly so after such a long period where it had been barely creeping ahead in misery. Joe was now desperate to stay alive. He felt a battle going on inside him and around him. He felt something fighting over him. He felt a war for his soul. He sensed a dark pit waiting for him, and something trying to pull him towards it; and he knew if he succumbed or gave in at all then he was absolutely going into that dark pit. But he felt something else fighting as well, something fighting with him, helping him to stay awake.

The war raged on for his soul. Joe contemplated what awaited him. He wondered if he would ever have a chance to live a righteous life. He felt himself slipping into the darkness. What was he going to do? What could he do? He didn't want to go to this dark pit that he could not see but that he could sense in a very real way. But he so desperately wanted to relax, give in, subside, and let it all be over. He wanted to sleep.

Summoning every reserve he had at his disposal, every ounce of energy, every bit of strength, Joe clawed his way off of the couch and somehow made his way to his roommate's room. He didn't knock. He just opened the door. His roommate was a heavy sleeper and never woke easily, but this time his roommate sat right up.

"What's up? Are you OK? What do you need?" Rob asked Joe.

Joe's roommate, his girlfriend, his family,

his friends, they all knew the state he was in, the situation he found himself in. They all knew how much pain he was in. He couldn't do anything he normally would do. He wasn't going to football practice or camp. He wasn't working with the players. He wasn't partying. He wasn't drinking. They all knew what was going on in his life, and they were all deeply concerned about him.

"Call an ambulance." That was as much as Joe could get out. Managing that had taken everything he had in him. But it was enough.

"OK," his roommate said. "Finally."

His roommate quickly called 911, and emergency services were dispatched. There was some small relief in knowing that someone was coming to help, and Joe was actively reaching out and asking for help for the first time in a long, long time. But still, Joe's pride held on. He knew he was dying. That absolute and unerring certainty of his imminent demise did not subside and was not fed by fear or pain or anything else physically going on with him. He simply knew in his soul that his time was now up. But he kept that to himself. He did not tell his roommate.

The ambulance arrived at some point. Joe wasn't sure how long it had been since they were called, but they were there. Joe concentrated on staying alive, breathing in and out, even though it hurt so much. When the paramedics arrived, Joe again let his pride take over, and he was able to muscle himself onto the gurney. He talked to the paramedics calmly, answering their questions, telling them his medical history. He kept all fear from his voice, and any that may have crept through would have been easily masked by the overwhelming pain he continued to experience. His adrenaline helped him. He outwardly kept this facade rigidly in place, even while he felt so terrible inside.

His roommate watched from the curb as EMS loaded Joe into the ambulance. He lay there on the gurney, staring into the bright, white, overhead lighting of the ambulance. He was now among professional, medical assistance. He felt that he finally had a chance. Should anything happen to him now, they would take care of him. They would make it alright.

The doors of the ambulance closed at his feet. The driver put the vehicle in gear, and with a subtle jolt and a hint of rocking, the ambulance started down the street. Joe breathed a sigh of relief and relaxed. He let go.

Immediately the ambulance stopped again. Doors were flung open. Lights went on. Paramedics scrambled giving chest compressions, providing oxygen through a squeezable airbag, and maintaining an industrious-yet-professional level of first response activity as they now took over the job of fighting to keep Joe alive. But they were losing this battle. Joe's heart had stopped. For five minutes and forty seconds, Joe's heart remained stopped. Not a beat was captured by any of the electronic gear hooked up to him in the ambulance.

Eventually, the paramedics rushed to close the doors again and the familiar red-and-white flashing lights bathed the street in their rapidly alternating, painfully bright pattern that flashed off the bushes and windows up and down the street. Joe's roommate swore. As the ambulance pulled away, he went back inside and grabbed his phone. He had several calls to make.

The Dark House

JOE FOUND HIMSELF IN utter darkness. He was awake. He was not aware of any transition. He remembered staring at the overhead light in the ambulance. Now it was dark.

He did not have an out-of-body experience. He remembered everything. But as soon as he sighed, as soon as he relaxed and breathed out, he was gone. In that instant, he woke up and found himself in this complete darkness.

He knew without a doubt that this was reality. Joe was not dreaming. He was fully awake and fully aware of his surroundings, except that his surroundings were completely and utterly devoid of light. Joe was still himself. He had the same body. He had the same mind, his same thoughts, his same consciousness. But Joe was paralyzed in the dark.

He could feel himself lying down in this darkness. He had complete sensory perception of every part of his body. He could feel his hands, his feet, his fingers, his toes. He simply could not move them. He could turn his head, he could move his neck a little, but it didn't matter. There was nothing to see, nothing to hear, nothing to focus on. He was stuck. The darkness was absolute without differentiation. It was darker than anything Joe had ever experienced before.

Over a period of time, or what passes for time in this realm, Joe became aware that he was in a room. He still could not see the room, but he became aware that the room existed. Joe lay in a bed in this room in the complete blackness. The room was very similar to a normal bedroom in an upscale suburban home, although quite a bit larger, and the bed that Joe was lying in was not the only bed in the bedroom.

In fact, there were nine other beds in this room. All of them contained sleeping bodies, except for Joe's bed. He was the only one awake.

The room remained in utter darkness, but the feeling or sensation of awareness continued to grow in Joe. He could not see with his eyes, but he felt the truth of the reality he was in. The occupants of the other beds were varied, but all were human. Male and female, young and old, they lay motionless, soundless, asleep in their beds in this large bedroom on the second floor of some home or building somewhere in utter darkness. Joe lay awake, terrified, unable to move.

He was unable to determine the passage of time. There was nothing to measure changes in the environment. No clocks ticking on the wall, no slow change of light, no insect crawling on the wall. He wondered if he was in some kind of hospital somewhere, but he knew he was not. He lay in the bed for a while, not knowing if it was minutes, hours, or years.

The door of the bedroom cracked open, and a sliver of light from the hallway pierced the darkness. It silhouetted the figures of two young women who slowly and quietly entered the room. Joe could see they were wearing scrubs. He wondered if perhaps he was incorrect. Maybe he was in a hospital after all.

The two young women entered the room, taking care to be quiet and not disturb anyone. They were young—very pretty, slim and curvaceous. Joe was startled by their presence. They frightened him, but he could not put his finger on why. He still could not move, so he pretended to be asleep as the occupants of the other beds were.

One of the women whispered to the other, "How is he awake? He should not be awake right now. He is not supposed to be awake. It is not time for him yet. He is not ready to see."

Chills ran down Joe's spine. Joe had been scared this entire time, but these words froze his very soul. The level of dread and horror that coursed through him could not be adequately described. If you took the worst fear you had ever experienced in your life, and multiplied it by ten, and then multiplied that again by a thousand, it would still be only the tiniest fraction of the fear that Joe felt lying in the bed. His entire being was fear, and it coursed through his body, up and down, drawing him into a pit.

The thought came to Joe over and over in desperation, *Move. You have to get out of here.* But Joe could not move. He was helpless in his fear. The two young women backed out of the room and closed the door tightly behind them, leaving Joe again in complete darkness.

Move. Move, move, move! You have to move RIGHT NOW! GET UP AND MOVE! You have to get out of here!

Joe found himself on his feet through sheer force of will. He didn't know how he did it; he didn't know if something perhaps released him, but suddenly he was unparalyzed. He moved with desperation brought on only by the deepest, darkest fears he had ever experienced.

He tore at the door handle to the room. It twisted normally, and Joe burst out into the hallway. His initial impressions were correct. He was on the second floor of what appeared to be a large house, but how he knew that while lying in a bed in pitch darkness, unable to see, Joe was unable to explain.

The hallway was short with a few other doors leading off it, and behind each of those doors was another room just like the one Joe had left, filled with beds and sleeping, uncomprehending bodies.

Joe did not wait to explore. He moved in the opposite direction, down a staircase to the front door. The front door was locked and would not open. Joe did not even attempt to try to unlock the door. His exit through it was barred, and he would not escape that way.

Continuing to move, terrified that he would not be able to move again if he stopped, he ran through the house, across the living room, and into the kitchen. There was a door there in the kitchen. He flew to the door as a man possessed. As he crossed the kitchen, he caught sight of the two women, the nurses dressed in scrubs, exiting another room just off of the kitchen. They saw him and gave chase.

Joe flung open the kitchen door and charged through into a garage. The overhead door was shut. He slapped the button on the opener mounted on the wall, but it did nothing. He knew that the door would not open for him. But there was a truck parked in the garage. A brand new, beautiful, tan GMC Sierra pickup. It was backed in, with the hood towards the garage door and the tailgate towards the wall that separated the garage from the kitchen.

Joe ran to the pickup. The drivers-side door was unlocked. He flung it open and jumped in, slamming it behind him. He looked for keys anywhere, in the cup holder, under the dash, behind the fold-down sunshade, nothing. This truck was his salvation, and Joe knew he had to get it started. He grabbed the steering wheel to peer over it at the dash and was instantly paralyzed again.

Joe felt the same as he had in the bed upstairs. He could not move. He had perfect feeling and awareness of his body, but it was no longer under his conscious control. He was paralyzed behind the wheel of the truck, grasping the steering wheel with both hands, rigid in the driver's seat. He could turn his head slightly.

The two women wearing scrubs emerged from the kitchen into the garage. They were not in a big hurry, but they were moving quickly. One of the women was taller than the other and had blond hair. The shorter woman was a brunette.

"I told you!" one said to the other. "I told you he was awake! He shouldn't be awake!" They stood just inside the door of the garage and Joe could hear them speaking to each other in frantic whispers, but he could not see their lips or mouths moving.

"Call Dad," the other one says. This provoked another new wave of terror to crash over and through Joe. "You gotta call Dad right now."

"I already did. He's on his way."

Joe didn't understand this. Neither of them moved away. Neither of them uttered any other sound that Joe could hear or sense. But when the one nurse said, "I already did," she meant that she had just done so. She had not done so before they entered the garage, but had done so while in the garage standing and looking at Joe. Joe hadn't heard anything and had not seen them move at all.

Now the two women nodded at each other and exited the garage back through the door into the kitchen. Joe's fear ramped up another notch. He sat in that truck, paralyzed, for another long while. He didn't know how long. There was no possible way to measure time. He sat in fear, wondering why he was there and how he could possibly get out.

After a bit, a man walked into the garage through the kitchen door. He was clean, very clean. He was not tall, maybe just below-average height, clean-shaven, neatly groomed, and completely unassuming. He was wearing faded Wrangler jeans, a flannel shirt with red, white, and blue plaid, and a puffy red vest over it all. His dirty-blond hair was starting to thin a bit and was cut short and combed neatly to the side. Joe thought he looked like he was in his late forties, maybe early fifties. His fair skin was tanned more than Joe's, but it was not dark. He looked kind and unthreatening, but the fear and terror that rolled off of him was intense.

"Hey, Joe. It's nice to finally meet you," the man said. He had a slight southern drawl, and he spoke slowly. His voice was mellifluous and smooth, rolling over Joe like he was the kindest gentleman he'd ever met. He had a voice that could sell water to a drowning man.

“Who are you?” Joe asked levelly. He was fearful beyond understanding, and he did not like that this person knew his name.

“You know who I am,” the man replied. “I’ve been with you for years.”

“I don’t know you,” Joe said.

He felt cold talking to this man, or this man made him feel cold. He didn’t shiver. The man just chilled his marrow. He could feel it in the pit of his stomach. There was no love, no humanity, no warmth in this being. There was only death.

“Why don’t you just come with me, Joe? You’re here. Why don’t you just come with me, and it will all be OK.” The man smiled fatherly at Joe. It filled Joe with dread.

“Sir, I don’t want to go anywhere. I want to leave,” Joe said. Being polite and respectful of this man seemed like more than a good idea. Joe felt it might be essential for his survival. “Where do you want me to go?”

“Joe, you know me. Would I steer you wrong?”

"You're crazy," Joe said. "I don't know who you are."

"Oh, you know, alright," the man said with a smile showing perfect, pearly white teeth. "Just come with me."

"Where are we going?"

"Just come with me, Joe."

This back and forth went on interminably. The man never raised his voice, never lost his patience. He just smiled, was laid back, and offered again and again for Joe to go with him. He never said who he was, and Joe never asked. Joe was terrified to the point of breaking as it was, and he was fearful of the answer of who this man might be. Joe suspected who he was as it was. He scared Joe's soul to the very depth of his being.

Joe didn't understand how he was able even to have a conversation with this man, he was so scared. The words were driven by something primal in him, through fear or adrenaline or something else Joe didn't know. Joe just knew he was scared, and that this man scared him even worse. He did not want to go anywhere this man might take him. Joe knew that if he followed this man, it was not going to end well. He didn't know what "not end well" meant in this case, but he knew it would be very painful for him. Whether that would be physical pain, mental pain, or something else, Joe wasn't sure. But he was certain it would be anguish.

After so many iterations and variations of invitations that Joe couldn't count them all, and with just as many polite deferrals from Joe, the man finally said, "I'll be back," and stepped into the kitchen and out of sight from Joe. Joe was left in the pickup, still frozen in place, both hands gripping the steering wheel tightly.

* * *

Now pardner, let's take a step back for a moment and consider Joe's situation back on earth. Joe's heart had stopped in the ambulance for five minutes and forty seconds. It took everything the paramedics could do to get it pumping again. They had performed CPR and pumped air into his lungs with a mask and bag, and once they finally had Joe's heart started again, they wasted no time getting the ambulance moving.

They called ahead to County Hospital to let them know they had a bad case on their hands, and when they arrived that small hospital did everything they could for Joe. They took blood; they ran tests; they took X-rays, but all of it was inconclusive. Joe was septic. It was clear that Joe was dying, but they didn't know what from. He was too big to fit in the MRI machine, so the doctors did the best they could with what they had available to them.

Joe was admitted and put in Intensive Care, and he was watched and cared for around the clock. He was on a ventilator, but his oxygen saturation was in the toilet and wasn't coming up enough. His heart was a problem. But Joe did not pass away. He lay in the ICU bed in a coma.

Over the next couple of days, Joe's family would all arrive and visit him at the hospital, and final arrangements were made. Joe's parents had been on a cruise in the Bahamas. When they had received the news, they disembarked at the next stop and flew back to Texas. They then observed their son in the ICU for days, watching him slowly die. It was clear to that family that the doctors were not optimistic about Joe.

Late one night, in the courtyard of the hospital, the family held a prayer circle. Tears fell, prayers were said fervently, and each member of his family did what they could to prepare themselves for Joe's inevitable passing from this world. Joe's mom spent the rest of that night in his ICU room with him.

Yes, Joe was in a heap o' trouble.

* * *

Time passed, or didn't pass. Joe couldn't say. He was left frozen in the truck for a period of time that may have been just moments or just shy of eternity. At some point, the man returned.

The clean, articulate, smooth-talking, friendly-looking man, the man that poured terror into Joe's soul just by his very presence, walked back into the garage. He was carrying two bottles of beer. These weren't just any beers, but they were two of Joe's favorite beers from a smaller brewery in Austin.

"Joe, would you like to have a beer with me?" the man said, holding one out to Joe. This was different from the conversation Joe heard from the two nurses. This man's mouth moved normally, naturally. He heard spoken language, not thoughts.

"No, sir, I would not like to have a beer with you," Joe replied.

Damn the man. A beer would be just the thing to settle his nerves right now, and this was a delicious beer. But Joe wasn't even tempted. The fear he felt at the man's presence and that grew worse with the offer of a beer was so overpowering that Joe felt no desire for it.

"C'mon, Joe, have a beer."

"No, sir, thank you."

"Wouldn't you like a beer, Joe?"

"No, sir, I would not."

"What's the harm in having a beer, Joe?"

"No thank you, sir."

The man offered Joe a beer a thousand times, and a thousand times Joe declined. The man offered a thousand more times, and still Joe declined every one. But Joe was beginning to become distraught. A man could only take mind-numbing terror for so long, and Joe had taken it longer than any man alive ever had. He was getting worn down. He wanted this to be over. On roughly the forty-thousandth time the man asked him to have a beer, Joe became exasperated.

"How can I even have a beer with you?" He glanced at and nodded towards his hands that were glued to the steering wheel. Suddenly they both fell free.

"Now you can," the man said with a smile. "Why don't you take this beer? It's ice cold."

Joe paused. He paused for a long time. The man stared at him intently with a warm smile on his face as he held out the beer to Joe. Joe looked at the beer. He looked up at the man and then back to the beer. He wanted for this to just be over.

Turning his head, Joe looked straight ahead through the windshield of the truck.

"No, I don't want a beer," Joe said at last, softly. "I want to go home."

"How do you know you aren't home?" the man asked.

The fear, the terror, that this man might be truthful, and the implication that Joe might never leave this place beat upon him. It beat at him and crushed him beneath an infinite weight.

"This isn't my home!" Joe said.

"You sure?" the man asked. The threat came through in his voice, even as his voice was soft with an upward lilt and an almost quizzical tone. His tone mocked Joe as the intent threatened him.

"Yes, I'm sure," Joe replied in desperate exasperation.

"How do you know you're sure?" the man asked. "Have a beer with me."

"No."

The man stood for a moment silently and then shrugged one shoulder at Joe. "I'll be back," he said. "Hands on the wheel."

He snapped his fingers, and Joe's hands were immediately grasping the steering wheel again. He was once more frozen in place.

Joe began to believe that he was in worse trouble than he had feared before. He was so scared that he could barely think, and yet he never became numb to the fear. The fear just continued, fresh at every moment, and Joe started to believe that maybe this was Hell. Not hell with a little 'H,' but Hell with a capital 'H.' The "forever" kind of hell. And this was just the beginning. He was certain that wherever this man wanted to take him to was going to be worse than where he was right now.

* * *

Back on earth, over a period of about a week, Joe's condition had not improved. However, Joe did not pass away. He remained relatively stable, maybe worsening a little, while his body continued to cling to life as it succumbed to some unknown ailment. He was in septic shock, but from what no one could make hide nor hair of.

One of the nurses felt some kind of connection with Joe. He was only thirty-four years old. He was in terrible shape and had clearly made some poor life decisions to be where he was, but she was certain that no one deserved to die at only thirty-four. She gathered another nurse and a couple of orderlies, and together they put in motion a plan to try to determine what it was that was slowly killing Joe.

They wheeled Joe down to radiology. There

was an MRI machine that allowed for a patient to sit upright. Joe couldn't use it. He couldn't sit, he couldn't stand. The nurses and orderlies were determined, however, and rigged up a stand out of some mattresses and beds. Together, they manhandled Joe into position. They held him in place while the radiology tech did her work scanning Joe's body with the alternative MRI. It wasn't as hard of a job as it would have been two weeks ago. Joe had lost a lot of weight as his body consumed itself while it fought to stay alive.

The results did come back, and they were good enough to tell the tale. One of Joe's lungs was completely filled with fluid. He also had moderate fluid buildup around his heart. That last was bad, but not yet critical. The lung, however, was worse than terrible. It was most likely the source of the septic infection and needed to be dealt with immediately.

County Hospital made quick calls to all their pulmonologists and cardiologists. The only person in the entire county who was certified to perform the surgery needed to drain the lung could not be reached. He was not answering calls, and no one could locate him anywhere. Joe needed intervention right now, and there was no one at County Hospital that could help him. If they didn't do something to make a difference soon, Joe would never leave the hospital alive.

The verdict was unanimous. Joe had to be transferred to Big City Memorial Hospital in Houston. Getting him there was going to be a large problem, however. Joe was too big of a man to go in the Life Flight helicopter, and he would not survive the many-hour trip in an ambulance. He needed more care than an ambulance could give.

More calls were made to a few connections, and another alternative and slightly unorthodox plan was put in motion. In less than an hour, Joe was taken by ambulance to the local airport.

At Podunk Municipal Airport, Joe was wheeled in his hospital bed into a chartered airplane and flown to Houston. His mother accompanied him, packing his body with ice and desperately trying to keep him cool, and alive. His fever spiked as the plane waited for insurance paperwork to process before they could receive clearance and take off.

Finally, they were given green lights. The flight was as uneventful as it could be with a large, naked man dying in the back while his mother tried to keep his body cool. Upon arrival and landing in Houston, they were met by another ambulance and taken to Big City Memorial Hospital.

The Chase

THROUGHOUT THE PREVIOUS TWO conversations with the man, the two women in scrubs had not been present in the garage, but Joe could feel or sense their presence. They had remained nearby in the house. After a while, they both returned to the garage with the man.

The man was dressed differently this time. He was now wearing mid-length swimming trunks and nothing else. His body was fit but not overly muscled. He looked like he took care of himself, but he was not a specimen of physique. He had a smattering of blond chest hair.

The nurses were still wearing their scrubs as they entered the garage. Once inside, both women slowly and exotically stripped off their scrubs and undergarments. Their bodies were as perfect as Joe could have ever imagined. Both were voluptuous, gorgeous, stunning women. They were perfect tens, and no woman he had ever met had ever had bodies like these two. Even the most beautiful of women paled in comparison to these beings.

The man smiled and gestured towards Joe and the pickup. Oddly, the roof of the cab Joe was sitting in was now the bottom panel of a large aquarium. Looking up, Joe could gaze into the cool, calm waters and see various fish and aquatic life. Joe loved the water, loved the ocean, loved pools and aquariums of all kinds. It looked relaxing, peaceful, and inviting. It filled him with dread.

There was no rational explanation for this aquarium to suddenly be there. It hadn't been there before. It was clearly still the roof of the cab of this tan GMC Sierra pickup truck. And yet it was real, too. It was every bit as real as the truck Joe was sitting in. It was every bit as real as Joe himself.

The two nude women walked around the front of the truck and opened the passenger-side door. They both crawled into the seat next to him. Joe remained paralyzed, his hands frozen to the steering wheel.

Joe could smell the two girls as they sat next to him, smiling and giggling at him. They smelled sweetly of lavender. It was a pleasant scent, and they wriggled suggestively at him. Thankfully, they did not touch him. Joe was relieved at the lack of physical content. The thought terrified him. He didn't want to be touched by these beings. He was certain that would be very dangerous for him. Joe knew enough to know right from wrong, truth and good from evil. It would not be good for his soul or long-term existence to be involved with these people.

First one girl, and then the other, dove from the seat into the console between the front seats of the truck. Diving in, they appeared in the water of the aquarium above Joe. This was not surprising to Joe. He could see how time and space were twisted here, and it made perfect sense. It was a bit of a show, to illustrate what they could do. He could look down on them through the truck console, and up at them through the roof of the truck cab.

Looking up, the two girls playfully swam in the aquarium above him. They looked down at him and motioned for him to join them. They swam freely in the water, making no effort to breathe or surface, and apparently had no need to do so.

"Hey Joe, you like what you see?" the man asked casually from the doorway of the garage.

"No, I... I have a girlfriend," Joe stammered.

The terror had not abated even a hint. Instead, it was ramping up. He had a girlfriend he desperately wanted to get back to. He would do anything to see Anita smile at him again, to feel her warm embrace.

"But you like to look," the man said, knowingly.

"I would never touch," Joe said.

"It's OK here, Joe," the man said. "You see anybody else here?"

"No," Joe said.

"Why don't you just get in the pool?" the man asked.

"I can't," said Joe, looking at his hands still glued to the wheel.

"You can move if you get into the pool," the man said.

Joe knew it to be true. And he was tempted. He did love the water. He liked to drink in the water. Maybe he could have the beer, relax in the water, not touch anything, and just let the man say his piece and get it over with. If he didn't do anything wrong, then there'd be no harm and no foul, right?

But the fear remained. The terror. And Joe declined again.

Over and over and over the man asked, patiently, for Joe to get into the water, and Joe declined each time. The girls overhead swam together and began engaging in foreplay. The man grinned and asked again if Joe wouldn't like to get in the water and have a pleasant time.

"No." Joe's denials were becoming simpler, shorter now. Just 'no' over and over again. The man now jumped into the pool himself, gesturing to the women and inviting Joe in.

"No, definitely not," Joe said.

The girls began engaging in pornographic acts, and the man joined in. Joe was repulsed now. There was no temptation remaining. Human-shaped body parts moving and engaging in inhuman ways, doing physically impossible things, smearing together and losing coherency. They regained human form and then temporarily lost it again. It was as if creatures were playing at having human bodies and didn't quite understand how they worked, having never been human. These beings moved like human dolls made of jello. It was grotesque.

Through it all, the man was somehow able to continually ask Joe if he would like to join. The refusals were adamant. Joe continually replied in the negative. It became clear to Joe that while it still felt like they were talking to each other face to face, they were not. Communication was happening separately from their relative bodily positions towards each other, and Joe's perceptions appeared to be independent of his actual body placement as well.

Joe's denials did not stop. They become automatic, without thought. Just 'No,' repeated over and over again. Time dragged on in its own unique fashion here. Joe was weary. He would do anything to be through with this, rid of this place. He felt like he had been in this house, stuck here with these beings, for at least a year. He was again tempted to give in, just to make it stop. He wanted desperately to be gone from this place. His soul was weary, fearful, and despairing. Joe knew he could not give in, could not stop denying these temptations, or he would be forever damned. But he wanted so badly for it to all be over.

Suddenly, and without transition, the truck was back to just a truck again. The aquarium was gone. The women were gone. The man was standing at the very front of the truck, dressed as before with the flannel shirt and vest. Joe was still paralyzed, both hands on the wheel. The man was staring back into Joe's eyes, yellow irises glinting malevolently at him.

There was no friendly, laid back, amiable look on the man's face now. He slammed his hands down on the hood of the truck, denting the hood as his fingers clawed into the metal.

"WHYYYYYYYYY NOOOOOOOOOOOOT?" the man howled, his face now distorted into a rictus of hate, lust, and avarice. His human features were still present, but now he looked demonic.

"WHY NOT, JOE?" he shouted. "Why not now? Haven't I always been there for you? Haven't I always provided you with willing, young flesh whenever you desired?" His lips and nose were curled and wrinkled in a snarl. His brow was drawn down, and his teeth snapped and bit out his words. "Haven't I always provided you with pleasures, whatever you desired? Women, food, drink, diversions of every sort? WHY. NOT. NOW?"

All of Joe's fears up to this point were trivial compared to this new onslaught. He could not withstand it. He cowered in terror even as he could not move.

Joe had never really prayed before in his life. He still didn't know how to do it. But he knew, now, at this point, there was nothing else he could do. He understood that his only possible salvation would come from God above, and without God, he would surely perish at the hands of this demon.

Joe just started talking. He bowed his head

as much as he could while still frozen and bound to the steering wheel and let the words just flow from him in silent, still desperation.

"God, I know I have never called on you. If there is any way you can help me right now, I need your help. Can you send somebody? Can you send Jesus? I need your help. I call upon you in the name of your Son, Jesus Christ. I need your help right now. Please, I am yours, I submit, whatever it takes, I don't care, please send someone right now..."

The engine of the Sierra instantly roared to life, the tachometer needle springing up on its own and dancing with the red line as the sound of the engine revving filled the garage and drowned out the shouts of the demon. The truck quivered and settled on its suspension. Joe's hands sprang free from the steering wheel. He jammed the truck into gear and floored the gas pedal. In an instant, the demon disappeared, gone completely before he could be impacted by the truck, and Joe rammed through the garage door and out into the street.

* * *

In Big City Memorial Hospital, Joe was still fighting for his life. Still, the staff knows more about what was wrong with Joe than anyone had before, and they hadn't lost him yet. There were four teams of doctors caring for Joe now: Critical Care, Cardiology, Infectious Disease, and Pulmonology. They all went to work taking care of Joe, each team handling what they could. First up was a CT scan, but lying flat for it taxed Joe's heart to the limit. They were extremely worried about his ability to survive any surgery.

The surgery to drain Joe's lung was a success, however. It was the last procedure of the night, the surgical team squeezing Joe in at the last moment. It took several hours, and Joe had a long, thick needle pierce his lung. That needle was attached to a hose that drained into a bag. Slowly fluid, puss, and effluvia started trickling down the hose and into the bag. Samples and cultures revealed it was digestive bacteria in the lungs with no indication as to how the infection may have happened.

Over the next several hours the nurses had to change the bags several times. When all was said and done, they drained seven full liters of fluid from Big Joe's lung.

Joe, however, still did not improve. His condition deteriorated and his vital signs became weaker. Joe's fever reached 105.7°F, cooking his brain. A cooling blanket covered Joe, and his body was packed in ice in the hospital bed.

The doctors wanted to perform another surgery to remove the fluid surrounding his heart, but they did not believe that it was likely Joe would survive that surgery. They held off, waiting to see if his condition would improve, but it did not. Sonograms and other tests revealed nothing. His heart rate remained irregular and rapid, and his fever continued even with four antibiotics, and now an anti-fungal, coursing through his body.

Even though Joe wasn't getting better, he wasn't getting any worse, either. The family transferred down to Big City Memorial Hospital in Houston and set up camp there, rotating shifts to be with Joe in his ICU room. The family was told not to touch him, as he was in really bad shape, and they were afraid to contaminate him further with something that might finish him off. They were also told to touch him and talk to him often, to let him feel their presence, to let Joe know that they were there. Confused and worried, the family had nothing to do but wait.

Joe's girlfriend, Anita, drove down Friday evening after work and remained with Joe's family during their long vigil of praying and waiting for a resolution. She stayed with them the entire weekend, only leaving late Sunday afternoon to return home for work.

Another day passed, and another. They risked another CT scan, and it nearly killed Joe.

His oxygen saturation dropped to 72%, and he lost even all involuntary control of the right side of his body. The scan was aborted. They performed a bronchial scope to see if there might be additional pockets of infected fluid in the lungs but could not find any. They could find no reason for Joe to not be improving.

The critical care team decided to try a trans-esophageal echocardiogram. It showed the fluid buildup around the heart, but revealed that it was worse than previously seen in the MRI. The cardiology team decided to risk heart surgery. Joe might not survive it, but he wasn't going to survive much longer without it either.

Once again, the surgical teams went to work on Joe. They removed thirty-three ounces of fluid from the pericardial sack that surrounds Joe's heart and installed another drain.

* * *

Joe burst out of the garage, gripping the steering

wheel tighter than he had when his hands were frozen to it just moments before. He ducked as the wreckage of the garage door fell to the ground around the tan pickup.

The driveway of this house was short, and Joe hit the street hard and fast. To his left, in front of the house, was another large, black pickup truck. It was equipped with off-road tires and a roll-bar just behind the cab. The roll bar was not chrome, however. It was pitch black.

The black truck was waiting for him, and as Joe hit the street, the other truck leaped forward, engine revving and tires screaming as they laid down thick trails of tread on the pavement. The headlights came on, as did the lights over the cab on the roll-bar. They were penetrating lights blazing out in the darkness, making the rest of the darkness seem even more total and complete.

Joe could see at least ten men in the truck, some upfront in the cab, some standing in the bed looking over the cab, and the rest sitting in the bed. The men all looked alike. They were big, tall, muscular, white men wearing white t-shirts, cargo shorts, and Red Wing shoes, with socks pulled up past mid-calf. They all looked angry and filled with hate, and Joe knew they were ready to fight. He knew they were looking forward to it.

In his life on earth, Joe had encountered many people who were very similar to these beings chasing him in the truck. They were rough-and-tumble country boys who liked to drink and were always looking for a fight. Big Joe, being as large as he was, had frequently been a target for them to measure and prove themselves against, and he had fought many growing up. He hated and feared people like them. But these weren't people. Joe could see that their features were malevolent. They had murder in their eyes, and they communicated it with their evil grins, yelling and snarling and wrinkling their noses as they bared their teeth and chased after Joe.

Joe hit the gas in his pickup and tore down

the street. As he did so, another demon, very similar to the ones in the truck, burst forth from the front door of the house and ran across the yard towards Joe's truck. He was almost able to keep pace with the truck, and he hit the passenger-side door before he fell back as Joe accelerated madly. A strong smell of sulfur overpowered Joe.

Joe was stuck in some kind of residential neighborhood with no through streets, and he frantically took lefts and rights almost at random, not knowing where he was, desperately searching for a main avenue or arterial roadway to get out of this area and to where he could speed safely away.

The black truck chasing him made every turn he did, sometimes gaining ground, sometimes losing a bit, but Joe was never able to lose them. The demons kept their spotlights on Joe no matter how quickly he turned. The smell of sulfur did not abate, and the demons chasing him jeered and taunted him.

"There's nowhere you can go!"

"We're gonna f***ing get you!"

"Keep running, it doesn't matter! You can't get away!"

They laughed and screamed and roared at Joe, demeaning him, humiliating him, dehumanizing him. They were tormenting him, and they took great sport in it. Their rough, evil, sinister, and maniacal laughs were terrifying and demoralizing. Joe began to realize that they could catch him at any time they desired, and there was nothing he could do about it. He could surrender and go back and be damned, or he could push on and give them their sport. This was just a new form of torture for him, and he was not bettering his situation.

Joe had no idea where he was. Nothing looked familiar, and he just pressed on, terrified to stop. There were no streetlights. The night was completely dark, and no stars were visible—just empty darkness filled with endless streets of upper-middle-class suburban homes. The streets were a maze, and Joe continued to flee, not knowing where to go, which direction to head in; and it didn't seem to matter.

Street after street, passing house after house, this chase went on. There was no other traffic on these roads, and Joe blew through stop signs without pause. Joe drove and drove. He continued on for hours, maybe a day, knowing he couldn't get away, knowing he couldn't stop, unable to find his way out, unable to make any positive difference in his situation at all. Finally, at long last, he hit a main road, and turning onto it, pushed his foot to the floor on the accelerator.

The truck surged forward in spurts and hiccups, jerking Joe in his seat. The engine sputtered. A glance at the dash showed the fuel gauge hovering over a large, red E.

"Really?" Joe thought to himself. "I'm out of gas?"

He had no idea how long he had been driving. This chase might have lasted his entire life. He didn't think to look at how much fuel he had when the truck roared to life, and he had no idea how far he had come from the house where he had been held prisoner.

Joe's heart sank. He knew what was coming next. He hadn't gotten away at all. But as he shook his head and began to despair, he saw a gas station on the corner that Joe was fairly certain, just moments before, had simply been another dark house in this unchanging and eternal neighborhood. The gas station was an Arco AM/PM station with an orange and blue sign.

The black truck raced ahead of him and pulled into the gas station, and Joe followed. There was nothing else to do, nothing that could be done. Joe could find no way out of this, could think of no way to escape. The demons all jumped out of the truck and started walking towards Joe, their faces dark as they sneered and leered as they approached. The smell of sulfur was choking.

Joe was desperate, but this time he knew what to do. Once again, Joe reached out to God.

"God, I know I just called upon you very recently, and you got me out of something. I know it was you. I'm yours. I have submitted. I am whole-heartedly submitting to your will, whatever it may be. I'm in. Please help me figure it all out later, but I need your help, right now."

Without warning, from out of nowhere, a fire truck screamed into the gas station, lights flashing and siren blaring, tires screeching. The truck leaned hard on its suspension as it turned tightly and braked fast, coming to a stop between Joe and the demons approaching from the black pickup.

In the rearview mirror, Joe saw two police cars pull up and park directly behind him, their lights blazing.

Large firemen jumped off the firetruck or climbed out from the engine cab and began to engage the demons from the black pickup truck. The police officers emerged from their squad cars and joined in the fray. Then more officers, and more officers still, step out of the black-and-whites. Joe couldn't believe how many men were squeezed into these squad cars. It was like watching a clown car at a rodeo. They just kept coming.

Relief flooded through Joe, and he exhaled deeply. The firefighters and the cops were quickly subduing the demons, but the demons had a lot of fight in them. It was a pitched rumble, but one that only one side was going to win. In minutes, demons were being thrown to the pavement, restrained by officers who were placing them in handcuffs and holding the demons in place on the ground.

One demon was slammed face-down onto the hood of Joe's Sierra. He looked up directly at Joe and smiled, his lips pulling back to reveal more teeth than belong in any human mouth. The teeth were long and sharp, each one coming to a point, and there was more than one row of teeth. The demon's yellow eyes stared into Joe's, and he felt hatred, rage, and mirth in his gaze. The demon was cuffed and yanked away. As another demon was paraded back to one of the cop cars, he, too, turned and looked at Joe. His eyes were completely black. They were dead, flat obsidian. There was no white sclera visible at all.

Joe was shaken by the looks exchanged with the demons. He knew that somehow the differences in the eyes denoted various ranks among the demons. Joe turned and stared straight ahead, and a fireman jumped down from the back of the firetruck. He turned and looked right at Joe, giving him a big grin, and said simply, "It's all going to be OK."

The fireman took a step closer to Joe and stretched and flexed just a bit. With a whoosh, two large wings sprang up behind the fireman. They were brilliant, beautiful, radiant white wings, and they banished the shadow of the night. They shed light all around the man, the angel, as though a spotlight were trained on him from a helicopter hovering above.

"It's going to be OK," the angel said again.

"Thank you," Joe whispered, bowing his

head and closing his eyes, overcome with relief at this rescue. “Thank you. Thank you.”

Joe felt the angel walk up to the truck. The angel tapped lightly on the driver’s side window.

“You can open your eyes,” he said softly to Joe.

Luke

JOE OPENED HIS EYES, turned to look at his rescuer, and realized that he was no longer in the pickup. He was standing in a lush, green garden. It was beautiful beyond words and stretched as far as he could see, with trees, flowers, and bushes. Far in the distance arose rugged, blue mountains. There were big white clouds in a perfectly blue, crystal-clear sky, and the colors... well. There were more colors than Joe had ever seen, ever realized there could be: Colors Joe had never seen before, colors no one on earth had ever seen before.

A refreshing breeze caressed the petals of flowers and the leaves of nearby trees. The breeze flowed past and through Joe, embracing him and strengthening him. Joe felt renewed and invigorated. He felt at home. He felt at peace.

Joe was more at home here than he had felt in years. It felt to him as comforting, friendly, warm, and as filled with love and anticipation as waking up on a Saturday morning did years ago when he was just a boy. The sun would be low in the sky and rising fast and Joe's dad would be cooking pancakes and bacon for breakfast. After breakfast they would watch college football together and spend quality time in each other's company. It was an immensely soothing feeling, and Joe felt as though a tremendous weight had been lifted from him. He breathed deeply, sighed, and relaxed.

Joe looked at the angel, and the heavenly being was no longer dressed as a fireman. He was radiant, tall, masculine, and the most beautiful being Joe had ever seen. He was strong, powerful, utterly competent, but unassuming. He was clothed in a simple white cassock. His wings sparkled like diamonds in the sun, and he smiled a broad, warm, friendly smile at Joe. His brown eyes glowed with a love and warmth and humor that Joe had never encountered before. It made Joe feel as if he were no longer alone, as if he would never be alone again.

"Man, Joe, it is good to see you!" the angel said. He reached out and put a hand on Joe's shoulder. It felt exactly like meeting a best friend who hadn't seen him in many years. "Really good to see you!"

"Yeah?" Joe said, confused.

"Joe, it's OK man. Everything is going to be OK."

"Who, who are you?" Joe asked.

"You know who I am," the angel said. "I've been with you your whole life. You just didn't know I was there. I've been with you as long as you have been alive."

The words made no sense, and yet, deep down, Joe knew them to be true.

"Are you my guardian angel?" Joe asked, awed.

"Finally! You get it!" the angel beamed at him.

"What's your name?"

"Luke," the angel said simply. "Man, it is really good to finally get to talk to you!"

"It is really good to be here," Joe said. "I didn't like where I was."

"I don't think anybody would," Luke agreed.

Luke and Joe talked for ages. They communicated not with verbal speech but directly, almost telepathically. It was direct, soul-to-soul communication, and it conveyed much more than words alone can. Meaning, thought, emotions, clarity, all came through instantly, and there was a fullness of understanding that couldn't be achieved with mere words.

Joe and Luke had very similar personalities. They meshed perfectly and felt completely comfortable with each other. They were instantly best friends, and they understood each other perfectly. It was an unexpected pleasure to speak with someone who truly understood him. Luke knew every thought, every desire, and everything that Joe had ever done. They walked in the garden for ages talking, Joe asking question upon question. He asked about Luke, his duties, his influence.

"Are you really my guardian angel?" Joe asked again. The whole thing was so hard to believe.

"Stop denying me, man!" Luke said in jest to Joe. "C'mon, man! How much more do you need?"

"Is this place Heaven?" Joe asked.

"Here? No, this isn't Heaven," Luke replied.

"Then where is it?"

"Someplace else. It is a different place, a place of waiting."

"Really? It's all real?" Joe asked.

"You knew it was real the whole time," Luke said. "You were just always afraid. You have to stop living with so much fear. You have to... if you go back."

"If I go back?" Joe asked.

"You have a shot, but it's your choice," Luke said, turning to Joe. "Do you want to go back?"

"When you say go back, do you mean go back to where I was, or to my earthly life?" Joe asked, suddenly trepidatious again.

"Joe, I love you, and I'll always love you. But that's not my call. You have to make that decision," the angel said. "And if you decide to go back, I'll have to go make a phone call."

"What do you mean you have to make a phone call?" Joe asked.

"Well, do you want to go back to earth?" Luke asked.

"I think so..." Joe said, almost with an edge of hysteria to his voice. He felt certain that there were only two choices. Joe knew that if he didn't go back to earth, he would die and face judgment, and be handed back over to those demons he had just been rescued from. "I don't want to go back there."

Luke sighed and grinned at Joe. "Alright. I'm going to go make a phone call."

He disappeared in a breath of air and the flutter of a feather, leaving Joe alone in the garden. Joe stood and contemplated everything he had been through. He was anxious, maybe even a little fearful, but he was no longer terrified, and his mind raced.

Gosh, I want to go back. I hope I get to go back. I need to see my girlfriend; I need to change my life; I'll do whatever they ask. I'm not going back there, I'm not living in fear anymore, I'm submitting, I'm theirs, I'm His, I'll go to church. I don't know what church to go to. Maybe I can ask Luke about that when he gets back...

Joe walked and thought in the garden alone for what felt like several hours. It seemed to go on forever. He encountered a small stream gurgling contentedly to itself and meadows filled with flowers. There were hills, and trees, and everything was arrayed so naturally and yet so artfully that it was absolutely perfect. Joe would not have minded staying in that place forever. It was more beautiful than the most gorgeous and impressive gardens on earth.

Joe had quite a bit of time to himself in that place. While Luke was away, Joe was visited by several relations. He was able to see and spend time with his grandparents on both sides of his family. He had never met his grandfather on his dad's side before, and there was a great deal of catching up and pleasant conversation. They, of course, knew all about Joe, but Joe learned a number of things from them that he had not known before. He heard new stories about his family. It all gave Joe a new perspective and understanding about his own life and his own direction, and what he needed to change.

These reunions did not go on forever, pleasant as they were, and to each of his family in turn he bid joyful farewells. Joe was left in the garden again for a time.

After a while, Luke reappeared suddenly and asked with a smile. "Are you sure you want to go back?"

He seemed to enjoy teasing a little bit, building suspense playfully with humor. Joe had done the same with his students many times.

"Yes," Joe said.

"Are you really sure?" Luke asked again.

"Yes," Joe said, "But I've got some more questions for you."

"I kinda figured you might," Luke confirmed. Joe felt that Luke knew everything that Joe wanted to ask or say before he said it. "But if you are going to go back, you are going to be charged with a task. This is a stipulation of going back."

"OK," Joe said.

"Whenever the opportunity presents itself, you are to share your story," Luke said. "There's no quota of souls you have to save. There's no scoreboard or tally you have to meet. You aren't responsible for any of that. You aren't a savior; you aren't an angel; you aren't a prophet. But whenever the opportunity presents itself, you are to share your story. You aren't responsible for converting anyone. Just share your story. It'll all be OK. If people listen, great. If people don't believe you, it's OK. If you're persecuted for it, it's OK. You know the truth. Simply share your story." Luke laughed. "And your physical story is going to be a pretty impressive tale on its own. You are going to go through the most difficult, most excruciating trials, mentally and physically, that you have ever been through."

"OK," Joe said simply.

"Are you sure you want to go back?" Luke asked one more time.

"Yeah, I do, yeah," said Joe. "I'll go through the physical thing you're talking about. How bad can it really be, compared to what I've just gone through?"

Joe sighed. "It's all real. Jesus is real. God

is real. The devil is real. Everything is real," Joe continued. "OK. But if I go back, what church do I go to? What do I practice? What do I do..." Joe said, trying to get it all out in a rush. "I don't know how to do any of this."

Luke laughed and shrugged. "Who really does?"

"OK... well... but..." Joe paused. "Where do I start?"

"Joe, if you do get to go back, it is never a bad idea to start with the original."

"The original... are we talking western religion, eastern religion? Do I need to start practicing Buddhism? Taoism? Confusiciousism? Are we talking Western religion? Do I need to become a Jew? I'll learn Yiddish. Do you want me to learn Yiddish? I can study the Old Testament."

Joe was a history buff, and all the various sects, practices, and religions of all the peoples he had ever taught his students all came flooding back through his mind. Joe knew history. He knew the stories of most of the religions on the planet. He just hadn't ever believed in any of them.

Luke held up his hand to slow Joe down. "The original," he said.

Joe started to ask about 'the original' again, but Luke spoke first.

"Joe, do we ever just give you the answer?" Luke asked, one eyebrow raised and a huge smile on his face.

Joe laughed. "No," he said.

"Ponder that," Luke replied.

"OK. Well, can you give me anything else? I'm going back. I'm in, and I could use the help."

"Good," Luke replied. "I'm glad. I wasn't certain you were in until you started asking me some of these questions."

"Can you just give me a little hint?" Joe asked furtively, shrugging his shoulders slightly. "Just a little one?"

"How about the Universal Church," Luke said.

Joe had no idea what the Universal Church was. He had never heard of this, but he wasn't going to argue. He'd been given his hint that he had asked for.

"OK, whatever, dude, uh, I'm in," Joe said. "No, I mean, not whatever, I'm sorry, I just mean..."

Luke laughed. "Joe, it's OK man. We love you. You're fine."

"You're sure?" Joe asked, almost plaintively.

"Yeah," Luke said warmly. "Joe, it's going to be OK."

* * *

"Joe, it's going to be OK." Joe could hear the voice from a great distance, coming through a great fog. It was his father's voice. "It's OK, Joe. Your heart is strong. It wasn't your heart. It's going to be OK."

"It's going to be OK, Joe." He could hear his

sister's voice on his right-hand side. That couldn't be right. His father and his sister hadn't been in the same room in eighteen years. Something wasn't quite right.

"You're going to be OK, Joe. I have to leave, but you're alive. You're going to be OK." It was his sister talking again.

Joe struggled to open his eyes. Everything was blurry. He couldn't talk. He was on a ventilator. He couldn't move. He could only listen.

"It is June 28th, Joe. You've been in the hospital, in a coma, for three weeks, Joe, but you're going to be alright."

Joe knew his experience wasn't a dream. It never felt like a dream at the time, and it never felt like a dream once he regained consciousness. The memory of it has never faded. It remains as perfectly clear now as it was when he experienced it, not even becoming less distinct over time as normal human memories do.

During Joe's life-and-death struggle and recovery, his family was brought closer together than ever before. His father and his sister were able to patch up their relationship. And Joe told his parents stories from his grandparents that no one on earth could have known. The impact was profound, and each of his family was moved deeply. Their individual faiths were rekindled and strengthened.

Over the years, Joe has even found that most of the details of his experience were more than simply the background elements of the reality he found himself in after his death. There was usually some meaning behind them, and Joe kept discovering little pieces, or perhaps they were revealed to him, as Joe shared his story and learned about his new faith.

The doctors never did figure out what happened with Joe's back pain, that symptom that had started everything a month prior. It may have been caused by the pericardial effusion or the pulmonary edema. It may have been something else entirely that resolved with rest while Joe was unconscious in his hospital bed. He'll probably never know.

Joe was in the hospital for months after waking up. He had to relearn everything all over again. And let me tell you, I do mean everything. He lost a significant amount of muscle due to atrophy while he lay in a coma for weeks. It was a major milestone when he could first move his arm only six inches off the bed. His mom took video of it, she was so proud of him.

"Show your dad what you can do," she said.

Joe's girlfriend, Anita, made the long drive every weekend to be with Joe and his family in the hospital. She was an integral part of his emotional support, and he needed a lot of support. They grew closer together than ever during these trying times, building a strong bond and a foundation for their relationship, and, eventually, they would be married.

Joe had to learn how to breathe again on his own. Moving, walking, talking, all over. He was like a baby. Eating, chewing, swallowing, even pooping, he had to relearn. After spending several months in the hospital, Joe then had several more months going through physical therapy. It will be years before Joe was back to where he had been before he tweaked his back, if he ever recovers that completely.

Even now, Joe has constant, burning pain in his legs, nerve pain, and he wears braces on his legs to help him balance and stand. He doesn't have much of any other feeling in his feet or legs. He thinks the pain is part of his "penance," part of his ministry. It is a constant reminder of where he was, and what almost happened to him.

He even thinks of his pain as a blessing. He feels it keeps him focused. And every time he tries to tell his story, this story, it drains him. It tires him out completely. He relives the entire ordeal fresh and anew. Before Joe tells his story, he has to work up to it. And when he tells it, he relives that inner torture, the fear, the despair, the loss, the damnation. Every time, he relives it. He feels the fear in his heart, in his soul.

That's my favorite part.

Joe thinks he's safe, and he is, for now. But he won't always be safe. I'll get him. I'll get him back.

I've got houses and houses full of souls just like him. I've got nurses taking care of them all, under the best care we can offer. We keep them sated and safe, calm and asleep. I'll get all of them, just as I'll get you too.

See ya soon, pardner.

Made in the USA
Middletown, DE
06 November 2020